Tea, Cake and Tears

ZOË HICKERSON

Tea, Cake and Tears

Copyright © 2020 by Zoë Hickerson.

Paperback ISBN: 978-1-952982-41-5
Ebook ISBN: 978-1-952982-42-2

All rights reserved. No part in this book may be produced and transmitted in any form or by any means, electronic, or mechanical, including photocopying, recording, or by any information storage and retrieval system, without permission in writing from the copyright owner.

The views expressed in this work are solely those of the author and do not necessarily reflect the views of the publisher hereby disclaims any responsibility for them.

Published by Green Sage Agency   10/15/2020

Green Sage Agency
1-888-366-9989
inquiry@greensageagency.com

Contents

Redux 1

Under Pressure 3

White Noise 4

Status Quo 5

Awake for a Thousand Nights 6

Devil Woman 8

Visa Waiver Programme 9

Looking at Me Looking at You 10

Complacency 12

The Finger of Disrespect 13

A Picture Tells a Thousand Words 15

Something Soothing 17

I've Felt This Way Before 18

Twilight Zone 20

In the Cold Feeling Warm 21

Eyes and Lines 23

An Educated Guess 24

By Dawns Early Light 25

Last Train Out 27

Española 29

M.I.L 31

Tomorrow Never Dies 32

Have a Lovely Day Sweetheart 33

Bitter End 35

Retardation of My Feelings 37

Don't Stand and Stare 39

Bursting the Bubble 41
Annus Horibilus 43
Flying the Flag 45
You're a Fraud 46
Tumbling Down 48
Economic Downturn 50
Imbalance 52
Committed to a Cause 54
I Can See Right Through You 55
Everything Happens For a Reason 56
Dutch Courage 58
I Will Wait 60
What's Your Poison 62
Sensual Pools 64
I've Lost My Independent Spirit 66
Humbled 68
Listen Without Prejudice 69
Critical Thinking 71
Modus Operendi 72
Low Tolerance 74
Returning to Sender is Never Guaranteed 75
I Salute You 76
I Will Go Quietly Along 77
I Thought I had Dementia 78
Odd One Out 80
If You Believe 82
Butterfly Kiss 84
Healing the Scarred 86
Holy Cow 87
Change in Manifesto 89

Tears of a Clown	90
Benevolence	92
Sabrage into a Bottle of Bubbly	93
Don't forget me	94
I Have an Angel	95
My Habitual Fix	96
Child's Play	97
Left out in the Rain	99
I realise it isn't Me	101
It's Never Really a Friendly Place	102
Tea Cake and Tears	103
Final Curtain Call	104
Bully Tactics	106
Goodbyes	107
In the Midnight of My Years	109
Sitting Comfortably in My Rear View Mirror	110
Save Yourself	112
Acceptance	113
Missed Connections	115
She Loves Me She Loves Me Not	116

Redux

I see a pattern here
I'm repeating it all again
I've become unhappy and disillusioned
I retreat within to find a way out
What does that tell you?
I can't keep on track?
Or our time is done?
I keep it secretive
It only makes it more decorative
When the truth comes flying out
I don't feel guilty
I don't feel bad
It shows how impulsive I can be
It shows my organisation is back again
I see a pattern here
Am I making a huge mistake?
I never seem to learn
One will never know until it happens
I know I'm repeating the same behaviour
I'm not doing my self any favours
It's worked out before
This time I have more self-awareness
So I will have to juggle carefully
It seems I never learn
And put everything on repeat

I can't always live with the deceit
I come out the other side relatively unscathed
With my screwed point of view
Making promises never to do it again
Here I am with this dilemma
Making others hurt forever
I'm going to have sit back and watch
Everything exploding around me
This is where I try and tentatively convince myself its right
When others say it's wrong
I've gone and made a huge pong
Redux

Written 1/3/2018

Under Pressure

I've gone global
I've put myself under pressure
It's kind of exciting
It's all very nervy
Am I going nerdy?
I'm a pressure cooker waiting to explode
Grey matter spewing forth
There goes her temporal lobe
There goes her cortex
Under pressure to explain myself
Under pressure due to the anxiety
How will I be perceived?
Or is it me being deceived?
That I'm going global
To push that final hurdle
Into the literacy world
We shall see
We will go with the flow
If the pressure gets too much
Who is going to give a bunch?
What happens to those who have a message to give?
Fuelled by alcohol and drugs
They end up on the carpet with a great big thud
Diseased psychotic and paranoid
They go into that death defying void
Oh lord
Fuck me
My inner demons come out to the fore
I've never been under this type of pressure before

Written 1/3/2018

White Noise

The fan in the bedroom
A coolness
The white noise I feel comfortable with
You are asleep
I am awake
What else is there to do?
Other than listen to my inner voice
That I do have a choice
No turnover to hold me tight
I guess this is it for the night
I feel rejected
I feel unwanted
I feel empty
What do I do?
Think to myself it never happens
The fan in the bedroom
A coolness
Comforting white noise
What do you want me to do?
Lie back?
Sit and cry?
What do you want me to say out loud?
There is no tension there
I don't forget
I string it up on an imaginary knot
How many of these do I have
I'm really sick of the rejection night after night
It's just me and the coolness of the fan

Written 10/3/2018

Status Quo

I want to die
I want to cry
I have lost that focus I once had
I don't understand anymore
Why do I keep going back?
Why do I go sideways?
Why can't I go further forwards?
I want to cry
I want to die
Please help disrupt my status quo
I can't see living as the only choice
I have my voice
I see snippets of how wonderful life can be
They are out of reach
When things go wrong
It makes me a necrotic wretched sole
Blowing stuff out of proportion
Just one day of perfection
Just one day of reflection
It would make me so happy
I want to die
I want to cry
I want to disrupt this status quo
It's one way or the other
Don't keep it dangling
Don't keep it hanging
For me this is the only future I see before me
Dying painfully
Dying unhappily
Please disrupt my status quo
It's whatever I want
It's whatever you can give

Written 11/3/2018

Awake for a Thousand Nights

I've been awake for a thousand nights
Wishing you be here for one of our delights
Across sand sea and vast wastelands of snow
I will surely know that you are coming back to me
With your sensual perfume wafting in the wind
I get a whisper of it when I know you are close
It has this smell that makes me weak at my knees
The sensual smell that sets off all my pheromones
Our hair standing on end waiting for that sexual explosion
I've been awake for a thousand nights
Experiencing that moment
When we are just one with each other
The world moving slowly around us
As I gently stroke your skin
Finding delight in every crevice
Your legs muscular and powerful
I am engrossed in all of your sensual sexual being
We are frenetic in our movements
You are my heaven

You definitely have my heart
Just to have that one last taste
Just to have that one last kiss
Before I am awake for another thousand nights
When you have gone
All I have left to remind me
Our perfumes a heady mix of togetherness
The distinct smell of sex lingers in the air
Our clothes strewn in disregard lay across my floor
Lying in bed the warmth of your body still emanating
My last sight of your beautiful body
As you gracefully walk out the door
Knowing I have to lay awake another thousand nights
Before I am awoken again from the dark to
Lay some delight to your pudenda
These are the days I truly remember

Written 12/3/2018

Devil Woman

I've swept that to the floor
It ran out the door
Many moons ago
I use it as an example
That stuff changes quickly
One day feeling sickly
The next up to your ears in an unforgiving mess
Stressed up to your eyeballs
Everything hunched into a tiny space
You see it drained from your face
If I had a crystal ball on the table
I would use it to enable
My capabilities that used to be higher than the sky
Then you can't dwell on the past
As you will end up last
As the black took cover
Beware that devil woman who has evil on her mind
She used to be
So nice
With a vice like grip
With a snarl on her hare lips
With ice in her veins
Treat her with kindness
Don't give her an encore
She doesn't need encouragement
As repeat performances are her thing
Her opening first night was critically acclaimed
Then the final curtain call
Gave rise to her fall
She fell flat on face
Oh what a disgrace
Be careful what you wish for
As you skate on thin ice

Written 15/3/2018

Visa Waiver Programme

Death has taken one again
Sad news
That makes you muse
The suffering they were experiencing
No matter what steps you take
You can fake your own wellness only so much
I can see you think
I can see the cogs wiring around your head
Actively thinking
I can't jump on board with this
It's too soon
It's too raw
It's making me claw and drag myself around
My head fluffy and full
Of all the family stuff
I'm not going to go the same way
No matter how perfect it may sound
I don't want to be found
With a noose wafting in the wind
I stand resolute
I know it can waiver
Like an American Resident Alien Visa
I wish you well
This is how I cope
Writing as you know
Is very cathartic
Learning how fragile life is
And it's the name badge
That only separated you from me

Written 15/3/2018

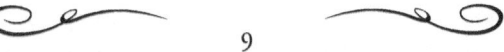

Looking at Me Looking at You

When does it start to become a problem?
Every time you look in the mirror
Deep down
You don't see
What others do
I've never asked
Not because I can't be arsed
There is a different me looking back
Why do I say to that?
Can you see anything strange?
I'm not estranged
I'm not deranged
Do you ever see me looking at you whilst I'm looking at you?
I wonder
While I wander through life
We know there are mountains to climb
Many rivers to cross
Which one will eventually become the boss?
I turn away wondering what happens to the other me
Do I become that reflective part?
Looking at me whilst I look at you
You can't tell me your secrets
As you never listen
Just a shrug of shoulders
Whilst I throw a boulder down the hill

Do I follow?
Whilst I wallow
In expectation of being chucked over the ledge
Anticipating the speed of gravity to tip my over the edge
Will you come after me?
Or will it still be the case
Looking at you whilst looking at me?

Written 17/3/2018

Complacency

I don't like it
I don't like how it feels
This is how I've been managed by my meals
It's my complacency
I'm bothered about
It sets you up to fail
It sets you up to put the final nail in your coffin
I can make excuses
I can make a fairly tail
I'm self-aware
I'm self-loathing
I'm conscious all the way through
Would it be easier if I didn't have one?
So why do we do it?
So why do I do it?
I've got to get on with no matter how I feel
I make a guilty deal with the devil
I make a deal to show I'm no good
All the food
He needs to drop me on my bum
In the end the wiring of my brain pings back and forth
Hold on a sec
Stop
Just listen
Listen to that shit
That's in your head
Stop wearing the complacency hat
Just get on with it and that will be that

Written 21/3/2018

The Finger of Disrespect

Do you have to let it linger
To show them the finger
Of disrespect?
The more time in your darkest hours
We realise how much was taken
Aching to make the time up is never easy
Taking care not to trip up or make yourself queasy
Sleep hygiene the most important tool
Because it can make a fool out of you
The migraine of evil gives way to the bottomless dark
As it hangs around in your dreams
Making no sense
Until you digress from the original plan
Sitting there digesting the horrors of the day
Do you have to let it linger?
Our memory plays tricks
As we get so dogmatic from both sides of the spectrum
Don't be so problematic to get lost in your neurotic days dreams
Show the dark the finger of disrespect
If your mindfulness tools crash to your knees
Who else is it going to please?
Other than the darks potent other half
Sniffing surreptitiously around your ankles
Fighting battles from all fronts
Get out
Move out
Disappear

I've only got room for one of you in hear
Unleash
Untether
Your inner fury
As you wonder why
I don't want to play your life changing dreams
Sometimes it's like playing catch up
Especially when I slip up
So here is my finger of disrespect
Every time you want to linger

Written 26/3/2018

A Picture Tells a Thousand Words

An image conjures up a thousand words
You can see the love pour out of every pore
Like the first sunlight of every dawn
Beautiful and unique
The stillness
Before the storm of
Unimaginable and unquenched grief
I can picture the horror
That stood before
Helpless
Hopeless
The silent bewilderment
Before the noise deafens in everyone's ears
A bone chilling cry
That a loved one can only give
Don't blame yourself
Don't please
It's easy for me to say
Because that is what we do
The what if's
The whys
The signs we miss
The cover ups that go unnoticed
We have a backup plan
If plan A doesn't work
Go to plan B
Visa versa

Until one of them does the job
I'm truly sorry
For being so blunt
Please don't go on the hunt
For people to blame
Only she put out her flame
People only come into our lives once
Sometimes for a day
Sometimes for years
To make a difference
Celebrate her life
Only you know the impact she made

Written 13/3/2018

Something Soothing

There's something soothing about being here
I know it must be you
The same time zone
The same city
A few miles apart
It's a pity we don't live much closer
That's my issue
When I need a tissue
There's something soothing
Knowing you're around
Balancing how much time to spend
It won't be enough in the end
That's my issue
Now I need my tissue
I wasn't confident about driving
I left it all to you
I wasn't scared
I wasn't doing my invisible breaking
I'm confident that the world is yours for the taking
It's been wonderful watching you grow and grow
I don't really want to go now
The time is coming fast
Where I will have to pack at last
Time is always on a slow
When we're many miles apart
There's something soothing about waking
up and doing the unexpected
Recollecting the places of my misdemeanours
Nothing is that familiar any more
That's my issue
When I need a tissue
I feel like a girl interrupted
My life was quite disruptive
I hope I made sense in my strangled farewells

Written 31/3/2018

I've Felt This Way Before

I've felt this way before
Not wanting to leave
Even though you have to go back
To?
Pay bills
Pay this
Pay that
To reality
Missing each other
Missing everything you accomplish
That feeling never really goes away
You feel it more and more
It's pushed under the carpet
Until it comes out the other side with more heartache
With other stuff you deal with day to day
It would be better if you had no connections
Then you wouldn't have those emotions
Empathy replaced with the harsh reality of sympathy
That come with
Filling your suitcase
Leaving your future behind
Somethings don't change
This feeling I've had before is harder to bear
Not sure if you wish to hear
Tomorrow we say our goodbyes
If I could make it better
I surely would
I've felt this way before
It doesn't get any easier
Stopping and listening to the nonverbal clues
The nuances
The old school truancies

That you really want me around
How can I fix it?
When I don't have any clue
Patience is a virtue
I will just say I love you

Written 6/4/2018

Twilight Zone

Your body is in shock
When you've not slept round the clock
Same patterns of behaviour
Same feelings of being worthless
Looking sad
Feeling dejected
All this will be seen as a weakness
Not the unprenitable fortress you once were
Standing guard
Behind the facade
It's not always easy to bury the hurt
As there are always mountains of dirt
Creeping deep under your fingernails
Mixing with the toil of your struggles
Washing and brushing them away
They return
Again and again
Usually with nightmares and a different spin
The start of sleep where you feel yourself fall
This is the point where life meets death
Awareness of been shaken awake from the twilight zone
How do you keep yourself going?
Knowing
That one day
The tap of evil will never be able to switch off
You want to find the wholly grail
For that chance of enlightenment
Only knowing you're going to fail
When
Drip by drip
The black invades
How about a game of spades?

Written 9/4/2018

In the Cold Feeling Warm

It feels like a bad dream
I was with you last week
In the cold feeling warm
Seeing you develop into a human being
Is one of the best feelings
Knowing I'm missing out brings me to the floor
It wrenches everything to the core
Making us poor without communication
Making me weep with frustration
Why did I decide to live so far away?
Why do we make so many irrational decisions?
That cause almighty road blocks on the way
Reaching enlightenment isn't all that good
All it teaches is you're not any good
At sustaining life beyond the tip of your snotty nose
Why can't we see what life would be like?
In the future when we're young
You see the heartache
You see how effortlessly the mistakes can be made
A cloudy crystal ball
Hanging in the hall
Distortions of truth
Mirrors our lost youth
Why do we make these life changing decisions?
The thoughts and feelings in our own big prison
It's a life sentence
Without a get out of jail free card
Or
Forever on parole
It's all a bad dream
That's why we've thrown away the key
Overdosing on the frivolous

I was with you last week
In the cold feeling warm
So tender to touch
Too precious to let go
Why do we hurt ourselves so much?
Why are we so preoccupied when we can't converse?
It's like dying a silent death
That makes everyone so bereft

Written 10/4/2018

Eyes and Lines

What do you see when you look at me?
The worn lines of many dramas?
Or the furrowed of fun?
Which line are you drawn to first?
Around my eyes?
Or my tried and tested hands?
What do you listen for when I breathe?
The sigh at the end of the day?
Or tightness in my breath that I could be near death?
Do you see my eyes sparkle?
Or do you see the pain as they tear up?
When waiting for a flight on the long journey back
What do you see?
What do you hear?
Who laughs loudest?
When names are pronounced wrong?
It never gets tiring the more you hear
What do you look out for as we say hello?
Is it the same when goodbyes are said?
Do you look up and down?
Is it the slight acknowledgement?
When your eyebrows twitch?
Look at me now
How do I look?
Have you ever asked how anyone is?
That startled surprise
Eyes opening full of light
Welcoming
Do you see a quiver on my lip?
Or do you see where the lipstick has run into those craggy lines?
Don't pass judgment
As you may need me one day

Written 15/4/2018

An Educated Guess

How can you tell me if I like myself?
Is it the way I'm animated in conversation?
Or the way I put myself across?
It's taken a while
To give you a smile
Thinking that it's over
Swinging from post to post
Trying to avoid the hangman's noose
Building tenacity and strength
I've gone from length to length
To show who I am
I'm only just learning
Can you tell if I like myself?
Or should I frivolously throw away the key?
To where I knew myself best
It's an educated guess
My chest heavy from the pressures of what I might find
What would it mean?
For you and me
A lightness returning
The darkness turning its back
Looking back for the attention it once so coveted
I've put too many in their grave to fulfil my purpose
It doesn't get any easier
Each leaving a mark
Mine is there too
The beginning
The past
The now
The future is upon me
It's an educated guess
That's elegantly entwined in discovery

Written 30/4/2018

By Dawns Early Light

By dawns early light
I almost lost my life
What would have I said
Just before I lay there dead?
Leave me the heck alone?
I've cut myself to the bone
I have no wish to live
So therefore give me the right
To end my fight
In my funeral pyre
Would I be screaming in pain?
For me to shout that I was sane
Just leave me be
I wanted to see
I wanted to hurt
So I could live my life again
By dawns early light
I had given up the struggle
To earn a death defying cuddle
From the black insidious muddle
That was poisoning my being
From the freezing out
I don't know what it's about
I lay here confused
With the right to be bemused
What have I done?
What have I said?
What have you found?
I scramble around
Tip toeing carefully
So I don't upset the status quo
Am I scared?

Am I fearful?
Just in case I receive an earful
By dawns early light
It may be forgotten
That I feel so rotten
In other people's company
It's certainly imbalanced
My apologies for my compassion fatigue

Written 27/2/2018

Last Train Out

I think I'm losing control
A blind panic has set in
I thought I was sailing along nicely
My sails in tatters
As I limp up the garden path
My heart goes boom boom boom
Whilst my eyes open wide
My breathing is laboured and crackly
I don't want this to happen
I'm not at fault
I'm telling myself this
Before my head goes hiss
It feels horrid
To have such torrid emotions
I'm not in control of my head
I think this
I think that
I think I'm a stupid prat
How do I control these unhealthy thoughts?
How do I control my body?
I know it will assume
That I don't appear to care
I'm sorry there isn't any room in here
I'm not confident sitting in one place
I stumble around
I'm not anyone's clown
I can't get out if it
As I'm sure to be followed
No one going to see through this cowardly fellow
On the last train out
I will begin to scout
That
Yes it has come to this
A definite fork in the road
Come see me when I'm underground

Come sit at my stone
Place flowers if you wish
Just not Lillie's as my eyes will begin to itch
Tell me your story
I hope it's not too gory
Come wet or dry
I hope you're not too ashamed to cry
I will sit with you metaphorically
While you converse with me telepathically
It grew out of control
Like the weeds on my bed
Just remember where and what was said
It will be branded on my stone
That I got the last train out

Written 19/4/2018

Española

My head hurts
My body aches
I'm fed up with this internal verbal intercourse
Galloping up speed
Jumping the highest fence
Landing in the water jump
Face down
Arse up in the air
People jumping all around
Give me a reign
So I can get back again
When your number is assigned
You do your best not to get behind
At starters orders
Everyone at the same spot
It's how you guide your ride
To the other side
That sets you apart
You do something strange
For your thoughts to rearrange
Losing control
Why yes I speak Española
Nobody understands your verbal homophones
Who knew I was new to this type of disorganisation
My sanity
In its infancy
Running round in circles
Achieving nothing justifiable
Just a headache to some
An absentmindedly piece of chewed up gum
Just a blob on the earth
Forced to dispel the myth that I am worthwhile
I can make everyone smile
My face distorted in shape
Looking like an muddy ape

Nobody really cares
Until you look outwardly with help
A great big yelp heard by all and sundry
Your face lifts from the mud
As you slowly remove yourself from the crud
As your vision begins to focus
You notice an almighty cheer
That you are the favourite here
Money being waved
Your reputation has been saved
Crowds circling around
It's overwhelming here
Give her a cheer
Hola hola hola
We have our decider
She's going to be a survivor
Her knowledge will be a homage to those struggling out there

Written 19/4/2018

M.I.L

You scared me last night
I thought it was a home invasion
Or some special occasion
Laying perfectly still
I thought you must have the skill
To tip toe quietly along
Sorry you were wrong
I saw your profile side on
Floating near the curtains
I didn't want to look too deeply
As it was way to creepy
Instead I turned away
M.I.L
Your presence was still hypnotic
I thought it was a side effect of my antibiotics
You were clutching a blanket
Not making a racket
Silently smelling
You weren't doing any yelling
It must have been compelling
By torch I looked to find you
Nothing sinister in your place
I must have had a worrying look on my face
Oh M.I.L
Please warn me
When you want to make another appearance
Then we can make a clearance
I will place a chair
With things you want to share
Preferably not at 2 in the morning

Written 20/4/2018

Tomorrow Never Dies

I can feel the gravitational pull
As you gently manipulate me towards the wall
I can see you still want me dead
Not caring about me
Wanting to silence the violence in my head
Tomorrow never dies
It still comes again and again
I agree with the feeling
I'm doing everything I can to stop myself
From being peeled piece by piece out of my car
I don't have to go far
To do an awful lot of damage
It's like a beacon
With a slow deafening pulse
The closer I get the more I hear
The roaring in my ears
Tomorrow never dies
Maybe if tomorrow never comes
I will have extinguished my demons
Smashed them into the ground
With every pound of my flesh
Demons and humans
Undistinguishable
We will rise from the mess
By a gravitational pull
Away in the sky
No need to say hi
As X marks the spot
Where she lost the plot
The dark will be delighted
His numbers have been blighted by the survivors out there
For him tomorrow never dies

Written 23/4/2018

Have a Lovely Day Sweetheart

Some days are hard
Gaining that extra yard
To beat the black in your veins
It catches by surprise as its happening
When you feel yourself sliding into despair
You feel smaller and smaller
As you sink insidiously into your favourite chair
Your whole being shrinking
Why is that?
It's like a black mist coming over the horizon
Unable to dissipate
With the frogs in your hair
Each one exploding in your face
As you try to understand the human race
Slimy and brown
Their poison will make you frown
A bitter taste
Belching up acid
That incinerates your unstable core
These days are hard
With no little card
Saying have a lovely day sweetheart
My heart skipping beats
Never able to find a regular rhythm
To hold onto any sanity that could be out there
I abhor feeling anxious
I dislike being on the cusp of suicide
It's rotten
When your ship has a negative metacentric height
Giving up on its plight
Unable to hold anchor
My rancour on an all-time high

I feel sick that I've been here before
Not on such a larger scale
It's disappointing as I know what's happening
Why can't I stop at the first hurdle?
Before everything goes sour out there
All I hear is the chatter of teeth
As I go beneath
To beat myself up
For allowing my soul to float desperately out
You don't seem to listen to get it out of your system
My journey I feel is coming to an end
So shall we just park it?
Where you first found it

Written 23/4/2018

Bitter End

If it's a natural progression
Then what is it?
What am I progressing from?
I have anxiety building
Using techniques I've learnt
Seems to be holding me at the mo.
We all know
It could turn into a blind panic sometime soon
With laboured breathing
Rushing around achieving nothing
Not coping
If things could be sorted
Sooner
I'm not a spoilt child
I'm not an insolent teenager
I'm not a privileged adult
I'd call my self-cultured
I've had my thrills
I've enhanced my skills
If ignored I could be detonating my internal fuse
I'm sure I would be killed
Who would be billed?
To clean the mess
At least that's progress with a negative result
I don't know how I'm going to walk
Without the support
It's in a different building
Where they will be doing the concluding
I guess that's progression
Or simply convenience
Where everyone will experience the unease
I will feel the squeeze going on in my brain
Waiting for more of the meltdown to commence
Burn some incense to rid the smell of the drain
Let's get the CBT train

I don't care if it goes in circles
I can ignore
The furore
Going on around me
What the hell
I have to face it
Get it over and done with
Another notch on the wall
To prove to us all
Life is temporary
That we are worth it until the bitter end

Written 24/4/2018

Retardation of My Feelings

Do you think crying will help me feel?
Do you think tears will run down when I kneel?
Do you think having a good old fashioned cry?
Will help you reach the sky?
What is stopping you questioning your reality?
You must be able to notice the disparity
Thinking about the retardation of my feelings
Inner preoccupation
Will land you down the station
How annoying
Is my clawing
To reach over the ledge
To observe a beautiful day dawning
Not having to worry
How I feel today
Someone help me with this emotion
Tears on the cusp
Staying dry
Trying to cry
It's a human thing
Shows a retardation of my feelings
I feel ready
Let's get steady
Oh I can think of many things
That will get the ball rolling
Why?
I could shout
I could scream
I could cry and I can't
This flatness
Is boring
I'm better off snoring

Twisting and turning in my dreams
Telling me I'm falling apart at the seams
Read me a sad story
Show me a picture of your family
You see the love shine
It hurts to see
Because I can't be there
One day I will cry
For now I will look up to the sky
And wish

Written 26/4/2018

Don't Stand and Stare

Don't stand and stare
While I'm feeling disappointed with myself
We all know how anxiety effects the mind and body
Aching where I didn't know was possible
Now I know everything is plausible
I'm tired
Don't stand and stare
While I'm feeling disappointed with myself
The extremes
Brings me to my knees
My relief was mind blowing
As it pulsated through my veins
I could've drank some wine
I know one glass would go in one gulp
Gulps turning to large sips
Barely touching my lips
Barely touching the sides
Warming the cockles of my heart
Becoming fearless as I binged on more and more
Alcohol oozing out of every pore
Don't stand and stare while
I'm feeling disappointed with myself
That's not for me
I have learnt that my poison can be self-destructive
Working my way through it constructively
Is boring
Your no fun
Get a life
You've lost your spark
Whilst standing in the dark
One day life was fun
Then one day it wasn't

Don't stand and stare
While I'm feeling disappointed with myself
Somethings gone wrong
I want to sing my last song

Written 28/4/2018

Bursting the Bubble

You notice an unrivalled thirst
When you travel
To the bottom your own private lake
Drowning slowly
Looking up
Tranquil waters with the sun piercing through the pale blue
Sparkling reflections of light
Mirroring
If you look close enough
Don't bother coming up for air
As you will see
Your life playing before you
In no particular order
A memory floating by
You reach and grasp wanting to relive it again
Bobbing innocently
Tantalising close
Unable to live that moment so it can't be undone
Another guilt ridden
Another painful and forgotten
Trying to swat the hard ones away
Why won't the happy one come my way?
Floating idly
Teasing your nose as it gently touches your skin
All different shapes
I sense no urgency to come up for air
How am I not struggling?
Why am I so peaceful?
I look for clues
For me to amuse
Whether I'm alive or dead
My skin looking translucent
I realise I have jumped in headfirst into a menagerie
I am comfortable here
Floating along with my memories

I've failed in the real world its harshness spitting out the weak
Reality dawns as I want to speak
It has seduced me in unknowingly
The bubbles texture is soft and durable
I have no need to flap as I'm not curable
Perfectly safe
I'm floating on my own
The seed sewn
In a pool with my memories
It must be like this when transitioning to the spiritual world
Is this a dream?
All I want to do is scream
I haven't finished
How can I be banished?
Clues float down
As a single air pocket escapes breaking the surface
I have to figure this life first
For my bubble to burst

Written 30/4/2018

Annus Horibilus

What a 50+ year old thinks now
What the 21 year old did then
I went about it all the wrong way
I saw horror on your faces you didn't have to say
Throwing prestigious education in the bin
That wasn't my only sin
Your Annus horribilus proved correct
I ignored everyone's painful cries
I ignored them til I left
A week before Christmas
I flew across the pond
A phone call Christmas Day
Relived those fears
We were both in tears
It's not the same here
Knowing it won't be easy my dear
You know more than you let on every time a question pops out
It's been in my head for 35 years or there about
Never letting on about the disorganised chaos
Yes it has been my ethos
Not to say anything
That's where I'm paining
Never to let on
An Annus Horibillus
Went on for a while
I had to do it my own style
I was immature

That was for sure
Blindsided by adventure
Blinkered by my narcissistic nature
I was struck by my values
I was stuck in obstinacy to walk with my head held high
Yeah you think you know it
Yeah you think now how did I live through that
I wouldn't put up with that crap
Cheers for that

Written 11/3/2018

Flying the Flag

Abject misery is flying its flag
Has come for ride
Delicately screwing with your inside
First or last crossing the bridge
Loved to be woken from his idle slumber
Indiscriminate with who he rouses
Flooding into unsuspecting houses
Levees breached
Lives lurched into the unknown
Facing life all alone
Worry you not
He's not lost the plot
A white flag
A dainty white feather
Keeping the innocent all together
Come rain
Come storm
Come burst drain
The white of the conscious objector never wavers
Looking for the lost life savers
Until enough is enough
The spoils of war claims its prize
For those who believe in compromise
The feather waved
The last flag flying
Isn't what it seems
White crosses strewn across beams
The skeletal framework of humanity
Lessons learned will be integrated into society
Marks misery and lost hope
Despondency idles in first
As yet he is to do his worst
Misery has won this battle
Those who are left behind settle with unease
The ravages of misfortune never cease

Written 1/5/2018

You're a Fraud

You're a fraud
Your company
Leaves a tainted taste at the back of my throat
How did you get this broad?
How did this happen?
Going quietly along
It wasn't the weather
It wasn't the turn of events
How did you pull the wool over their eyes?
No matter how much it denies
Your credentials looked charming
No matter how alarming
You tried to be calming
Awash in a sick and twisted haphazard way
You took distain and grandstanding
To a whole new level
Bile stinging my taste buds
As all I remember is your contempt
With your attempt
To allay any fears
Yes you brought me to my knees
Yes you made tears flow from my eyes
You broke my spirit
You broke my resolve
I had to learn
I had to fight
You're a fraud that doesn't deserve the right to judge
I know you too well that you won't resolutely budge
Your slimy smile
Your silent stealthy approach
Your arrival
Made a fight or flight response
Making the hairs stand on end
As if they had been electrified
Your backhanded comments that had a positive and negative tone

I'm sorry you never reached the throne
I don't think that was your intention
As you placed everyone in contention
To fight amongst themselves

Written 3/5/2018

Tumbling Down

I'm not afraid of my world tumbling down on my face
I've been brave
To know I can end up in a grave
The signs are there
Pointing out where
It's not unique to think like this
It gets everything of my chest
Like thick green and sticky phlegm
An encumbrance for sure
Having it knocking on my door
I'm not afraid of my world tumbling down on my face
I accept it with dignity
I've been able to continue the race
I've seen others come crashing down
Worried frowns
As they try to figure what life is about
I've gone from the depths of despondency
To feeling it right back to my infancy
Learning
Yearning
Turning the corner
We try not to look behind
Through the rind
Of our thick skin
Put the pedal
To the metal
As we sing our favourite songs
Tuneless
Not clueless
As we were at the beginning
I'm not afraid of my world tumbling down on my face
Contorted in displeasure
I will have to measure
That I don't really care
As I did book my fare

It does come with a price
Because you go there more than twice
Each time a second or so closer
Towards the threshold of closure

Written 6/5/2018

Economic Downturn

There's been an economic down turn
Caused by a rampaging dogfight not far away
You can hear the screams
As I'm woken from my dreams
The horror is palpable
Left and right hemispheres battling for power
Fighting their way to their goal
There will be no retreat
Just me in the middle of no man's land
Deflecting shrapnel big and small
Bringing me to my knees with the greatest of ease
Home-grown terrorists plotting secretly
Detonating homemade bombs
Sanctions have been drawn up
No peacekeepers will want to stay
As the insurgents won't go away
Judges around the table giving their delivery
Their rivalry is incongruent
There's been an economic downturn
Caused by a rampaging dog fight not far away
A magical light show if you believe this be true
A bullet goes pop as it explodes through skin and bone
The persistent onslaught in my head wants a ceasefire
Just for some rest and regroup to patch things up
To build new tools for the pounding in my brain
Global warming and its greenhouse affect causing toxic rain
Making it difficult underfoot
A thousand white crosses stand in a beautiful spot
All with my name
As I've taken a dive from being alive
New ones made daily
Some sit idly
Until something simple washes it like new
There's been a rampaging dog fight not far away
Everything that I want is so tantalising close

I struggle tenaciously hour by hour
I don't know how to reach it
Everything has turned sour

Written 10/5/2018

Imbalance

Life is a balance
Between dark and light
When I don't come out of the fog
It gives me an almighty fright
Confusion leads to indecision
That I'm on the slippery decline
Everything spirals out of control
My control
It's a strange place to look out from
Because I know
My body tells me so
Life is a balance
Between thick and thin
The thin blue line
When you don't know what mood you're in
Breaking out from confinement
When my mind at its very worst
Waiting for something to burst
Brain cells
Tear ducts
Or even my heart
When all three come together it's time to go
I don't want to know
Just one is enough
Yes it gets really rough
Balancing life for the living
Or balancing death for the dying
Wanting to die as I can't see a way out
Frustration at not having information
Wanting to control is a huge factor
Not having the answers may seem trivial
What a load of drivel
Never being good enough
Seeking that praise
I've actually done something good for a change

Instead of rolling with mediocrity
Who puts us on such reverence?
Knowing that it was another chance gone begging
And that you're the last one in the class
Breaking fragile glass that was my ego
We're all human at the end of the day
Some have their wires connected a different way
That's why we're the black sheep
My life is an imbalance
We're not all working collaboratively together
It's ok to step out the box

Written 13/5/2018

Committed to a Cause

It's so easy to become disillusioned
When you're committed to a cause
To gain exposure
And put yourself out there
It's so easy to give up
To throw it all away
What's the point if nothing transpires?
It's so easy to become disenchanted
With things I've always wanted
I will find my own stairway to heaven
To master my potential
When you're committed to a cause
There's no way we should pause
To show true passion
In your own spectacular fashion
We all get there in the end
No matter how much energy is wasted
To write my trilogy
Without any resolution
When you're committed to a cause
And you've shown all your flaws
Such a rancid tang
From one of your gang
No wonder why we have difficulties
With our own peculiarities
Exhausted we stand
Divided we fall
Tell me is it really ironic?
That these words
Can make you feel so melancholic

Written 17/5/2018

I Can See Right Through You

Let the world pause for a moment
So us sinners can pray for atonement
Forgive me for my sins
It's breaking in the winds of time
So I don't have to slime my way out of redemption
I have to give into my temptations
I can't live so cleanly
You have to love me dearly
Wobbly and knobby bits seen so clearly
Let me pause for a moment
I can't see what I have done to deserve my power
I can see you cower in the distance
Stealthy you come
I'm not afraid
As we meet in the middle
I extend my hand in gratitude
A sign for you of peace and love
Talk to me once
Talk to me
I want to embrace the good and the grand out there
You stare right through me
I feel our brain connect as one
It is too much to bare
For you it is too late to care
As you can see the sinner inside of me
Too much heartbreak
My mind remains threadbare
Let the world pause
Let peace be insightful
It has to done by nightfall
Keep on walking
You may come promenading again

Written 23/5/2018

Everything Happens For a Reason

Everything happens for a reason
It's the reason we're put on earth to die
Everything happens for a reason
It blows with the season
One minute you have a talent
The next it's all gone
Blown away in the wind
You stand with your hands on your hips
And a perturbed look on your face
Something is missing
An emptiness inside
Wondering why has everything gone so quiet
Dumbfounded
Bemused
Why was I so confused?
These words are not mine
Holding them in the air
As a gentle breeze helps them float away
Everything happens for a reason
Why have I bought my self to treason?
I feel betrayed as this is not my goal in life
What was it that brought me here?
Who was it that steered me into this path?
No one can tell me
As my words come back to haunt me
Twisted scissors majestically playing indiscriminately
Until enough pressure exerts
Paper cut after paper cut
Stinging form the salty air
Words melt into the wind
Tiny specs of dust have no meaning
I stand on the edge arms out stretched

Hair whipping around my face
Gently leaning forward
As I float effortlessly towards the sand
I will be famous one day
Just not today

Written 23/5/2018

Dutch Courage

The end of the knife is crystal clear
I fear the end is near
One deadly slash
Would end my dash
Defeating my demons
Suicide a silent witness
It seems the perfect way to go
A measured stab through and through
My hand would waiver
Hay mate you want to do me a favour?
A casual slice
Will do so nice
I have knives here at home
So why the need to roam?
The end of the knife is crystal clear
I know my end is forever present
It just has to be drastic
I will pay you in plastic
Pay wave or Uber are the in things
If not what's the point
Standing around thinking about so many ways
One scar is too many
Just make your hand very steady
Go on its like slicing pork
Without the squeal of a drunk old Pom
My judgement impaired
I won't be cynical
I would make sure I wouldn't oink too loud
Just to make myself proud
As my belly would be full of beer

To make my ending a cheer
I will point to the spot
To give you Dutch courage
As you've probably had a lot too
Let's try stone cold sober next time
The smell of stale beer isn't to everyone's taste

Written 24/5/2018

I Will Wait

I will wait for you on the other side
I will wait patiently
Your life is still needed
For me I sauntered down this dazzling path
Sweet music all around
No melancholy
People dressed in the most vibrant purple you could imagine
Voluptuous females leaving nothing to be desired
Gliding along with open arms as their loved ones passed through
I will wait patiently
As I know your work is not done
I went before my time
As it was my life in the line
I saw no one was impressed with how I went
Careless was one remark
Deep deep sympathy was another
It wasn't in anyone's agenda
I just did it to cause no fuss
Of course you're going to remember
Like I do now
It wasn't one of life's big mistakes
I had a plan from early on
I tried to be strong
I tried to carry on
I know I kept it quiet
So not to worry you
Or put extra pressure to keep ticking along
I did it for a cause

Maybe selfishly so I could become famous for my work
I left life in the balance
I found that hard too
So I tipped the scale to my advantage
I will wait patiently for your arrival
Don't come this way too quickly
As the boss can be rather prickly
Take your time
Enjoy life
And don't think of me too deeply

Written 27/5/2018

What's Your Poison

If I find the time
Maybe I should drink your wine
It flows forth with spectacular ease
Red is my poison
My tipple
Perfectly scented as I raise a glass to my lips
I wipe it away
As my disinhibitions come into play
If I find the time
Maybe I should dine from your finger tips
It won't leave a stain around my lips
Food and drink the soul of our party
More often turning into a heady glaze
Will turn into an aggressive malaise
Don't turn your back
Otherwise you may feel the wrath of a drunken slap
This melancholy soul
Once so vibrant
Has turned into a transient wine vagrant
Wanting to feel the buzz takes longer and longer
The stronger the content
The more disconnected I feel
Stumbling around in an alcoholic haze
Forgetting that your reputation is at stake
Instead of thinking about that dried old grape
The alcoholic smell from the night before
All rancid and black
Time to change your values
Before dependency beckons
If I find the time

I will give back in kind
Not to be that dependent and broken old woman
Laying on an old park bench
Pigeons tap tap tapping at the vomitus stench
Rats gnawing on wizened fingers
Be careful outside as death lingers

Written 28/5/2018

Sensual Pools

I put you in my highest regard
It hurts when I can't think
It's tortuous when I sink
I have to think of myself stirring in your arms
As you tenderly stroke my hair
In a loving and passionate embrace
You are the most sensual person I have met
I have to let you go at some stage
We cling to the precipitous of love
It is frowned upon
And not in the cultural norm
I would run across red hot embers
Just for one last sizzling kiss
On your passionately engorged lips
I know it's too hard to let go
Our time has been a whirlwind of sexual explosion
I want to smell the air after we've had our affair
I love the way you talk
All sultry and sexy
I look wide eyed
Barely muttering a sound
If I could I would catch butterflies
Everything I am is because of you
Everything I ever wanted to be is because of you
Your disinhibition is fresh
You have taken me through orgasmic creations
Holding my hand whenever we go
It's like life slipping away on a vocal chuckle calling your name
As thunder and lightning reaches its climax
Slowly washing away
A beautiful smile on your lips
Invites me in for more
We dance entangled as our breasts clings together
The music slows
As we entwine further into each other as if we are one

Sweet sensual sweat pools in small indentations on your skin
I gently lick fervently
Until you have disappeared
I am not psychotic
As you are so hypnotic
We will definitely be here again

Written 20/5/2018

I've Lost My Independent Spirit

I've lost my independent spirit
I'm co existing in my head
Shackled by my own inabilities
It's a sad state of affairs
Finding that oomph that can set me free
It's how you feel after a double shot of espresso
It maybe gone but it's not forgotten
I think you can hear it in songs
The slower the better
Belting out your sad
Doesn't really sell that well
I certainly feel that raw emotion
Trying to break free
It's palpable
Just like my own heart
I feel broken
I feel sad
Trying to be in the moment when I feel like death warmed up
We have immaterial souls we can call upon
To guide us spiritually
They are not with us physically
Although there is an enriched earthly presence
We need to read our Angel cards and see what it says
I see it very appropriate for this time of day
I've lost my independent spirit
My feelings of self-worth
I can't stand the pain
It's a personal gain
To let go of what haunts you
It's a scramble up there
The more you remember
The more open and unfortified you feel

Consequently you build up again knowing what to expect
I know the effect
It feels harder somehow
Expecting to open fractures of emotion that flow over the top
Stinging my nose like I've snorted crack
The trees have closed their canopies
From the faltering light outside
I barely see my boots
How do we soldier on?
Without breaking completely apart
Swathes of forest are a comfort
As their voices rustle in the breeze
I don't feel safe
I don't feel at peace
Until I've told my final piece

Written 30/3/2018

Humbled

I feel humbled by your generosity
I feel humbled that you have to sit and listen
Listening without prejudice
Waiting for that passionate and eloquent person
You haven't seen before
Keeping up the momentum
Even when you're having a bad hair day
I feel humbled by your time
To reinvigorate my life
I've come to a major hindrance
A stumbling block
I can't seem to unlock
I don't have the power to keep this door open
It smashes me in the face
A cold wind has come to town
Opening and closing rusty gates
We all yelp frenetically
As it crushes our resoluteness
I've foraged
I've also rummaged
Down other alleyways
It still leads me back here
I know what I want to do
Each success is getting further and further away
My net gains
Just about outweigh my net losses
I've stumbled to an end
Where I see no light
I write to be coherent
I write with lucidity
If this is how it's going to be
I'm not going to accept that
I have enough hope to see my future

Written 26/5/2018

Listen Without Prejudice

A peaceful silence
A pin could drop into the ocean causing
A tsunami warning across the motherland
I'm present
And time has flown
I don't know what lies ahead
A week in bed is a major comfort
No work no play
Tranquillity
Hiding my
Exhausted vulnerability
Collecting my thoughts
Wondering if I will be like this again
You listen without prejudice
As we recall demons
A child sitting on a chair
Fiddling with her hair
It feels like I've had a tantrum
And I've been banished to the stairs
Impetuous and frustrated
The inner child has been stamping her feet
While her brother sits back in gleeful anticipation
Go the top of the stairs and don't come down
You know straight away that I will show my will
Silently sitting on the window sill
The lounge door closes with a thud
Every agonising second I will silently creep down
Showing poor judgement as I amble in
Back upstairs I drag my feet
Stay in your bedroom we will give that a go
Toys aplenty
Playing silently

Your brother playing sentry
It's always a conundrum why we forget
You listen without prejudice
I thank you for that

Written 31/5/2018

Critical Thinking

Did someone turn the dimmer down?
Or did someone blow out a match?
Its smoking away gently into the air
A pungent smell that some may like
How do we distinguish life?
When we lose hope
With the things we have accomplished
I'm barely able to raise a head of curiosity
Barely able to listen
Someone turned my life around
I can feel it on my skin
My hair becomes lifeless and thin
A burnt out tree
A burnt out me
Not a lot of difference really
Are we still living or sitting lifelessly
I'm hungry to spring back into life
To feel joyful
To have fun
How do we justify our existence when
Somewhere in the middle a jigsaw has lost its piece
Now I feel I will never get my act together
No critical thinking
I think
Then I cry
Is there a reason why
I need help with life's return
I feel embryotic
With potential for rudimentary development
It's elementary
I've probably left it too late
I should've kicked it a long time ago
Is it really worthy of such a lengthy wait?

Written 2/6/2018

Modus Operendi

With a brush of the wind
It could all dissolve tomorrow
With a simple mistake
I could come to a climatic end any day
Would I give a dam?
If it was abolished
Lability of mood
Thoroughly scrutinising myself in a disconcerting way
I want what you got
I know I need to remove these memories
It's proving harder than I think
Why has it stirred so much emotion?
I cried to work
I cried from work
I'm crying now
Tears turn to ash as they spread across my face
It's proving hard to continue
A brush of emotion strikes and I have to run
I want what you've got
What am I going to do?
I haven't even got half way through
Wait for the juicy bits
You have to hit the depths of despair
To be able to repair
I have to take ownership and manipulate myself back
I've invested in a lot of trust
To bust my gut
I feel sick with stress
I feel like checking out to a new address
I want what you've got in handfuls
I want what you've got in bucketful's
Jealousy is a dangerous thing
It stirs everything inside
Wasted energy
It turns to passion

A burning obsession
It erupts into hatred
Everyone has their own modus operendi
Hiring a PI
Watching
Listening
Furtively crawling through the undergrowth
Sitting and staring from every avenue
Only caught by the spit of saliva resting innocently on his chin
I want what you've got
I'm never going to get it
So why is it so important now?

Written 3/6/2018

Low Tolerance

I've got a low tolerance threshold
I've got a low tolerance for the mundane
Leave me alone
So I can get myself together
I know it's my maladaptive way of coping
Everything I say I think it's said with malice
I don't live in this ethereal palace
Everything I breathe will come out the wrong way
My fine motor skills letting me down
All I do is frown
With what spouts from my mouth
Is not my excuse
It's not verbal abuse
It's not carried out intentionally
I've got a low tolerance for bull
Indeed my social etiquette fails me
My language of manners is not what I'm used too
Why?
When it has been engrained in my character
I've got insurance to keep myself safe
In way it's superlative to be so pessimistic
I have the foresight to prevail
In my tenancy of this world
Who are the landlords who uphold the innocents to rights?

Written 5/6/2018

Returning to Sender is Never Guaranteed

You start your life with difficulties
It should be plain sailing from there
Nevertheless
What you put inside is rarely
What you get back
Every little blip
We seek reparation
I should have never had surrendered
It's the endurance of the manipulative
Who always come through
What about the rest of us showing strength of character
As we scramble and jostle awkwardly towards our goal
It's the survival of the fittest
In every human race
Returning to sender is never guaranteed
The runts of the pack
Are always pushed back
Last to get nourishment
Last to have encouragement
Always squashed and never promoted
First to leave the family nest
Ok we thought it was best you leave right now
To stand on your own two feet
We go about things in the most disorganised ways
Their idiosyncrasies make them stand out like a sore thumb
Their uniqueness never fully understood
Usually this unpredictability rarely pays
Their eccentricity squashed and ground to a halt
An entity in their own right
Returning to sender is never guaranteed
When your six foot under
Then you can stand your ground

Written 6/6/2018

I Salute You

How can you define courage?
What does it look like?
Some say they found courage
Doing their job in the line of fire
Another finding courage
To leave an abusive relationship
We all find it in some part of our lives
Some call it resilience
My type of courage is
Finding the strength to carry on with the living
Instead of bedding beside the devil
I've put my foot to the mettle
For me to be able to settle
Courage comes in all shapes and sizes
It knows no stereotype
We have to have moral strength to preserve
Otherwise it's wasted
What does it mean for you?
For me
Courage is also
Being truthful with oneself and admitting it
Showing your vulnerability
I have learnt
Not to be discouraged
We will have good days
Some days we will be in the dark,
Despondent and demoralised
Life is a compromise
Knowing when to let go of one futile battle
To carry on regardless
For all those courageous people out there
I salute you

Written 11/6/2018

I Will Go Quietly Along

Countless unhappy souls have taken their own lives
We wonder why?
Until we see how
They have struggled through pain and sorrow
We question again
Do we get a golden ticket half way through our living?
Stating how we die
It doesn't bother me
I will go quietly on
How many can foresee their future?
How many will slip past?
When someone says I can see you doing that
Will you be sad?
Will you be shocked?
When someone has made such an exhaustive
And intense impact in your world
Many a time I have thought I want to end my life
Especially when I can't see the way forward
I write because I can put my thoughts down honestly
It's truly liberating
The intense pressure moments you can't control
When everything explodes inside your head
I'm not jealous
When I see others liberating and unshackling themselves
I will go quietly along
If I foresee a time I will go marching on
I'm not unhappy
I'm not sad
I have been blessed
Many a time
Who knows what happens next?
I do have moments when I think why?

Written 13/6/2018

I Thought I had Dementia

Last week I thought I had dementia
This week I know I don't
Two different worlds
Work and relaxation
I can't seem to gently jell the two together
One makes me talk and have fun
The other makes me flap and look incompetent
Two different spheres
The left the right
I obviously look completely different
Tense and old looking in my distorted frame
Relaxed and looking younger
To find that hunger that has been stored somewhere
It's allowed out occasionally
Last week I thought I had dementia
It had me fooled
I had come unglued
This week and the next I know I don't
I must confess
From experience
We all must like living in a mess
How would we be if we didn't live in misery?
Nothing to complain about the drudgery of life
The perfect Barbie and Barbie
Or Ken and Barbie if you're that way inclined
I'm sure if they were real
They would feel the pressure
To conform in our cynical world
Where we build people up in popularity
Only to see them take nose a dive from the paparazzi
From the top to the bottom in seconds
Why do we do that?

Why do we want to see their misery splashed across the tabloids?
Then using the paper for our haemorrhoids
When I thought I had dementia
I was in my own little world
Trying desperately to grant freedom from my slavery
Ignorant about life
Only trying to figure mine out
Is that abnormal?

Written 14/6/2018

Odd One Out

Have I always been this outcast?
Have I always been this down and out?
I feel the odd one out
For some reason
It's easy for my thoughts
To think I'm the oddity around here
I don't look normal
To be able to look formal
I feel I'm the odd one out still
My oddities don't compare with anyone else out there
Right from the very start
I was given someone else's heart
A change of blood
To stem the flood of calamitous DNA
Is this where the odd begins?
I've always gone my route
No matter how futile it could be
I admit
I can pledge my allegiance
With my hand across my chest
I thought I was doing what's best
I've taken the high road
I've taken the highway to hell
Compared to others
I don't think it really matters
As we natter away about our individual qualities
The runt of the litter
Always sounds quite bitter
We may be odd
To some poor old sod
We've got there in the end
Some of us are still reaching for that pot of gold
At the end of every rainbow
We maybe outcasts
We're always reeled back in

With that familiar tone
Can turn our hearts to stone
Have I always been this outcast?
Have I always been this down and out?
Yes I have been the odd one out many a time
There must be some familiarities
Not to be thrown out of your house and home

Written 16/6/2018

If You Believe

If you believe in yourself
Then only you can set yourself free
That answer will always be there
It's the journey in between
Somewhere along the line
You will say it's going to be alright
It's a sudden realisation
With your internal conversation
Take yourself away
From the stress and business
Go find a spot where you can truly find peace
I found mine yesterday along the water
I know I will have to return
Back to reality
It's going to be formidable
If you can believe in yourself
With that ambition I can reach within
Feel that comfort
That said it's going to be alright
Maybe then I can move mountains
It's a dash of hope
It's a rush of inner strength
So I can hold it all together
Life is like a river
The main artery
Its little tributaries
Growth begins at the source

We all paddle down in our own canoe
The gentle splish splash
As we fight against the tide
The more we believe in ourselves
The easier it becomes
An epiphany from a photograph
I have an angel here and up there
Isn't it about time to give back?
Instead of take take take

Written 17/6/2018

Butterfly Kiss

Know this before I die
I will cry me a river
As I gently slither down the muddy slopes
My thoughts on tenterhooks
As I silently drift away
The mighty has fallen
I hadn't given up hope
Like those who smoke dope
Sublime butterflies gathering
Gently covering my face
Like a mother touching her stillborn child for the very last time
Give me a dime every time this happens
The unbridled emotion
An unenviable task of knowing when to take it away
I cry me a river
As I shiver
I dare not breathe
I dare not sneeze
I will exhale their dainty scales
Until I know nothing compares
Spreading death and destruction to something so fragile
Death is much bigger than I expected
It leaves others feeling rather dejected
Know this
From any final kiss
Make a warm embrace
To state your case
As it will be the final thing we remember
Before we set the final agenda
Know this before I die
There is nothing covertly wrong
We should learn to be more overtly forgiving
Death is just the start of a new dimension
Why so much tension?
We can walk in your shadow

We can be a comforting pillow
Look up to the clouds
An angel sitting close buy
Perfectly protected
Ready to give that first butterfly kiss

Written 19/6/2018

Healing the Scarred

I feel sad
Now I'm leaving
The relaxation turns
To desperation
I have no more to give
Where I live
It's a sad place
With sad and desperate memories
All places are time limited
We know this is true
The internal roller coaster begins again
How to stop the stomach churning
Broadcasting lies and untruth
I will have to find the real truths
If I'm in a place that's no good for me
How do I get out?
How do I go about healing the scarred?
I'm already broken beyond measure
You see it in evils pleasure
Oh how I wish to be
Unscathed
Untarnished
Unscarred
I'm already feeling pessimistic
There's a wall between two universes
You got it I'm there in the extremes
As sunset approaches
We have to make those decisions
I find it really hard
Healing the scarred
Over other scars I already have

Written 18/6/2018

Holy Cow

Eye to eye
Toe to toe
Don't let my imagination go
It can flow at the best and worst of times
It depends on what energy is released
Nothing happens
Like a ticking clock
It starts to flow
Like blood from a deep cut
Sometimes a scab forms straight away
Then I have to pick and pick until I get to the juicy bits
Other times it's like I've hit the jugular
Then it all comes gushing forth
Excuse the vernacular
I've got an image of the spectacular
I go straight to the point
Heart to heart
Beat by beat
I bet your good on your feet
Dancing and twisting
To the soul of our song
Hips gyrating
Wouldn't that be good in bed it's very fascinating
Not having to do the work
Reliant on you to do all the sweating
I will lay
Mesmerised
Eyes wide open
Pupils dilated
Caressing your beautiful bum
Goose bumps as you stroke my sweet spot
An almighty groan
As you give pleasure
Don't measure it
Just go with it for now

I will express holy cow
Let's do it again
Sated for now we will relax in the sexual after glow
Before we build up again for another steamy encounter
As you start crying for release
I ease your liquid tears
Salty and musky
You certainly make me husky

Written 20/6/2018

Change in Manifesto

I could guzzle my favourite drink all night
I could snort recreational drugs by day
Hey at least I won't be feeling much
My foundations numbed to my core
Smelling sour
Yes I could do all these things and more
Why?
I would be unable to distinguish
Between fantasy and reality
I would be decomposing before everyone's eyes
They both would delay my progress
Give me false perceptions that everything is ok
I would turn into a nasty drunk
I'm not good when I'm sky high
Why pour poison into your body?
When your thoughts are poisoned too
I would sit unaware
I would stand alone in my manure
Sifting and sifting trying to find the clue
I have been given the platform to change my manifesto
I will do all this stone cold sober
Why rob myself of this opportunity
I've put myself on a huge learning curve
To explore alternatives
To determine what is important in my life

Written 24/6/2018

Tears of a Clown

You can shout and shout until you're hoarse
It still won't show your remorse
The tears of a clown
Don't normally make people frown
How do you make it up?
How do I make up for lost time?
Knowing it was me who was mistaken
My tears tell me there is a lot of sadness and guilt
It's sickening to feel
I keep going on this big wheel
Building an armour of steel
To protect and to hide
From anyone going inside
Hopefully one day I will sit and prey
For the restart
These don't come along that often
So grab them while you're still cushioned
Tears of a clown will set you free
Go and pick the juiciest fruit from a tree
One two three
Take a break from these desperate thoughts
The past will haunt
The future is fresh and waiting
With your nearest and dearest
The things you fear most
As children learn
History has a way of repeating
Show them the love
Show the compassion
So you can have some common ground
You can shout and shout until you're hoarse
It still won't show your remorse
Tears are the sign
That you will dine with a different feeling each day
Somehow they cleanse

To moisten your lenses
So you make a difference with your every seeing eye
The tears of a clown
Won't make me feel down
I was dead back then
The injustice has aged me
I'm alive now
To put wrongs into rights
This living is really a fright to get the fight going on
If you've stumbled and tripped that's ok
It's the getting up and restarting with what
We have to empower ourselves

Written 27/6/2018

Benevolence

Today isn't the day
Yesterday day was
The day before et al
It's a stinker
My physic hunched
Everything could go crunch
Into the unknown
The known of the past
Not the knowledge of the future
We're creatures of habits
The easy ones we choose to wallow
I'm going to swallow
And sweep brusquely aside
This can't go any further
No secretive messages
No I spy with my little eye
No hiding in the shadows of humanity
Start with some creativity
Think of an outrageous excuse
Not to go back to work
This is what some of it's about
The others I can't do anything about
Apart from cry and look at photos
I've got the night shift blues
Even before I've started
It sits heavy right behind my eyes
I've misplaced my benevolence
It's cold
It's damp
Some days it's a camp
A five star hotel
I'm not doing this for infinitum

Written 30/6/2018

Sabrage into a Bottle of Bubbly

Who's going to win a prize?
For my termination of existence
When its 10 degrees below zero
No one wants to be my hero
Dress in a cat suit made of feline fur
Jump into the jokers wide eyed delirious grin
Sabrage into a bottle of bubbly
And I will tell you this quite subtlety
This prize isn't for the feint hearted
The snow drifts
Turning everything into a mirror
Don't deliver here
As you slide mercilessly along
The wind chill drops everything dead
A spade bashing the cold hard rock soil
They toil and toil
Until their blood boils
Venting steam as sweat mixes with the cold night air
Icicles hanging from their snotty nose
Hold on strike that pose
Let the winter wonderland pass
As you know it will
Spring into action
You will have more traction
Strike the earth it won't crumble under pressure
Unlike the owner who bores and infuriates in equal measures

Written 1/7/2018Don't Forget Me

Don't forget me

Even though I seem far away
Don't forget me
Even though I feel pretty close
Little things happen
That aren't always going to be clear
When you look up or feel a change in my breathing
That's when I'm shedding a tear
I'm finding today harder than most
I'm feeling a little vulnerable
I don't know what I fear
Please excuse me if I talk with a sneer
It's not supposed to happen
As I can hear myself perfectly clear
I'm not confused
I'm not sure if I'm that safe
What I really want is my own little place
It starts with an unusual feeling in my stomach
From there you don't need to guess
Don't forget me my dear

Written 3/7/2018

I Have an Angel

I have spiritual guidance
A reading that will bear fruit
I'm amazed with the truth
My dollar was wisely spent
I believe these cards were worth waiting for
Waiting for me to reach in and be touched
I thank you very much
I have been given the signs
I have been given the wisdom
Angels are always in our midst
I have an Angel there
Look square in the face
Look at the photograph
Not everyone can see
It's so there
We should learn from their touch
That when things are rocky
Life will get better with our power from within
It takes its time
Instead of thinking you're always at the scene of a crime
It's time to plug in
Cut the red for live or green for earth
It's not always so black and white
Exploding an anonymous package
Our Angels amongst the living
Have the capacity
To use their Incandescent love for life and to guide
To create a space
With a lovely embrace
I wholeheartedly believe
I have an Angel here
Nobody realises until towards the end
Don't drain their reserves
You get what you deserve

Written 6/7/2018

My Habitual Fix

My habitual fix
Has had a bit of a glitch
I can't look
I don't want to surmise
I don't want to speculate
As it will be me turning up late
It's not a triumph
It's a cold hearted tragedy
I can see myself in a fridge with a note wrapped around my toe
A sheet just about covering my nether regions
Even in death you have dignity
My heart will be misplaced
My brain in formaldehyde
How can it lay there while I'm still thinking?
I can't look
I don't want to surmise
It's a supreme surprise
How did I get this wise?
With time flowing
You will be knowing
A kick will drop me to the floor
How am I cope?
Without my habitual fix
The first thing I think is where that rope is
Blindingly turning out draws and draws
That could pin me to the rafters
Or nail me to the floor
I hope it's not true
Realistically what am I going to do?
The panic will give rise
To no compromise
What am I to do just sit there and shrug my shoulders?

Written 7/7/2018

Child's Play

You can sense the sadness
Around my madness
Way before you enter the room
It's a type of smell
That can't be dispelled
It has to permeate every nock and cranny
Before being thrown out by my nanny
It never leaves
As it swirls around the trees
Creaking and cracking their roots
Until it turns into dust
The type of dust we brush away
When children go out to play
We scorn as we shake
The red earthy dust stubbornly staying
Encrusting into the tiny lines of your hands
You can sense my sadness
As you wash it down the sink
That last obstinate speck as it clings on for dear life
Wash me away
With soap and water
I will try not pass it on to my daughter
One thinks we can cope
The other thinks not
That spot on the edge of your nose
As you look cross eyed at your toes
Distraction by laughing
As you go spinning around the room
The wind has blown
The rain has scoured holes into the ground
Dark muddled puddles lay in state

Just before we enter the gate
No dry patches to jump too
The only solution is to walk through
Creating patterns with our footsteps
Never let the inner innocent child break away
No matter how tarnished you feel

Written 9/7/2018

Left out in the Rain

You start your life with a blood transfusion
Is this the beginning of the confusion?
You think you are trying to make a better life
When in fact you're causing more strife
In your youthful head you think family is great
You presented me on this plate
I can make it on my own
My seed was sewn
In my journey of self-discovery
I've learnt now that family is everything
You make decisions thinking it will be alright
When it's not
You miss out
Your called different
Because all you want to do is keep moving
Moving from what
I've learnt that life is circular
All you do is return to the beginning
Where relationships were tight
Yeah you had a good fight
To be top of the food chain
Only toys and the dog were left out in the rain
You look out of the window and you wish can I go out again
What's so strange about that?

I've put my soul into this hole I can't get out of
I want to press return
It's easy on a phone it's just one click away
I wish I would have listened to those tears of others
I've discovered
When listening to mine
They are not from happy times
Now I'm stuck
With my memories good and the not so good
You all probably think I've had all the luck in the world
I can't fix the undone
What's done is done

Written 10/7/2018

I realise it isn't Me

If you feel vulnerable and lost
Don't come to me
I don't know what you're looking for
I realise it isn't me
I think my face has a bit of a snarl
I haven't felt right for a couple of weeks
That's no excuse
I'm having to push the boat out more
To tell the truth
I do worry
Maybe about all the wrong things
I listen to the way I talk
I realise it isn't me
Even the way I sound is peculiar
Why?
Is it empathy?
Is it Sympathy?
Are my priorities different?
Do I give authoritative information and advice?
If they are unparalleled
Why am I still questioning?
I'm hungry for knowledge
Just feed me and I will soak it up
I have to be cognisant of my professional boundaries
I sound cynical
Maybe I was nihilistic
Then only expressing it inwardly
Something has awkwardly sauntered in my place
I watch
I listen
I digest

Written 15/7/2018

It's Never Really a Friendly Place

It's never really a friendly place
All mixed up with twisted emotions
A place where obsessing and clarity
Are a never a good mix
For some a quick fix
Will do surprisingly well
For others you can never tell
A place of deep unhappiness
It's not really welcoming
A place of comfort is not anymore
A place of frigidity where it runs freely
As shampoo onto hair
To the observer looking in
It's never really a friendly place
I expect you see the same?
A silent shake of your head will give it away
I won't look your way
Because now I have to squirrel it
The fractured anxiousness waiting for something to pounce
Just see it from my side only once
It may help you decide
I vent my frustration not in the same vein
Put me on that train
Where the silence never stops
It's never really a friendly place
The inhospitable atmosphere can be sliced
Twice or thrice
I twiddle with my ring or my ear
How did we come this far
What benefits us?
When we have so many disparities

Written 17/7/2018

Tea Cake and Tears

The thought of happy relatives
You see them in pictures
You see them in the park
That love that they only know
An intimate touch of a hand
How they entwine in an embrace
The eye to eye contact shows love and devotion is for them only
The commitment so profoundly inspiring
Strikes down piercing my heart
A growl of
Wanting
Wishing
Moving quickly aware
It's rude to stare
With what they have there
The thoughts bring you to tears
Tears blocking your view
As you stumble
Into someone's stew
Profusely apologising breaking that attachment
The placing set for two
I knew you would be distressed
Would you accept?
Sitting with me
Tell me your story
Tea cake and tears aside
You see before me
That this will happen too
Stop running
Stop
Open your heart and soul
Let everyone see
Some days you feel it's a tragedy
It's ok to show your vulnerability

Written 6/7/2018

Final Curtain Call

How do I prepare myself for exit stage right?
When I've always got first night nerves
It's been a mammoth task
Learning about myself is a big ask
Some bits I can remember
Some I can't
It's done the world a favour
Unleashing me off the streets
Self-awareness
Coping mechanisms
I hold tight to my chest
Instead of a theatrical death
It maybe just PRN from now on
When I need a top up
Or a swift kick up my backside
I showed how vulnerable I could be
I guess I'm independent now
Even though I don't always feel it
Two sporting events held my focus
How did I stop the locusts?
From destroying all my crops?
Is it a sign?
In a strange way
I know I will cry
Especially when England won against Uruguay
I know I have bigger fish to fry
I hope it's not going to be my final curtain call
Letting go feels really strange
I really appreciate the change
Don't go begrudgingly from all that hissing and booing
Then you won't go grrrrr in your head
Goodbyes I find are never easy

They always make me feel really queasy
So I'm saying sayonara
We're worth more than that
I don't want any flowers
I want to feel your powers
Reaching long after the dust has settled

Written 19/7/2018

Bully Tactics

Abandonment isn't the nicest of things
When at you're all time low
It compounds the fact that you're no good
You become bitter and twisted
Why enlist when you have free range of armour in your head?
You know deep down
You know deep down that piling on all the black
Will keep going stack by stack
The abandonment you felt when the second kiss never came around
Or the harsh rebuff when appreciation is spurned
The look of despise
You can see it clearly in their eyes
The deadened feeling in your thighs
When shock roots you to the spot
And you only want to run and hide
Embarrassed by the redness in your face
The snigger
The haughty point of a finger
As they run away
Joined at the hip
By their childish little clique
You can see the sympathy from one of them
When they turn around shrug their shoulders
Your eyes meet theirs
The void left by expectations
The hurdles and hardships we face
The sadness we feel when everything is glossed over
With a tin of brightly coloured paint
No matter what our race
The knockdowns verses resilience
We should all be given a chance to progress
Abandonment
Rejection
Exclusion
It's all the same thing

Written 25/7/2018

Goodbyes

Who determines how we say our farewells?
Be it casual or formal
It always leaves me in a quandary
How long have I had this reaction to detachment?
I'm sure there's more like me
It's followed me through history
It even has name
Not that I'm out to shame
It's how I grew
It's how it grew to be so long
Never knowing I was wrong
A quick chirpy goodbye
No matter there or here
I don't want to see that emotion
It makes me feel uncomfortable
Why the rush
When all you want to feel is the hush
Before silent tear drops crashes
From the ashes
I'm able to explore
Even with my own self awareness
Even then my detachment
Is still unenviably poor
What do I have to do?
What do I have to say?
So long
I can't keep it in for long
I know the last words are the memories that stick
Like the physical closeness
I find it gut wrenchingly difficult to pry myself away
Then I know what you're going to say
Because I've done it wrong again

So long
Farewell my honey
You can bet money
That the final curtain will be drawn
When I least expect

Written 27/7/2018

In the Midnight of My Years

When snowflakes fall on your finger tips
A puff of cool air
Renders them motionless in time
I fear my sanity will be taken away
I fear my tears will fall silently unnoticed
A hole
A void
Nothing compares to this barren space occupied for so long ago
I feel the sting
I feel the warmth
As they gently melt
Gathering momentum as they cascade down my checks
Nothing shines like the midnight of my years
What has made me so emotional?
What has made me feel so blue?
I don't have all the answers to decipher
I know my silence will follow
In my catatonic wallow
I have escaped death by a hairbreadth
I feel
No warmth
No love
Just like my favourite glove
Alienated against the rest
The pain of longing never dissipates
The knowing ache
The thumping dullness
The ancient longing of moons past
When snowflakes fall on your finger tips
They sparkle in the sun
Rainbows of brightness
Glows in the midnight of my years

Written 27/7/2018

Sitting Comfortably in My Rear View Mirror

I've fallen out of love for the world
It turns my stomach into knots
The time when shoulders are hunched
I can't really give a bunch
As I'm concentrating on my inner self
Trying my hardest not let the dark rule
It's the cruellest part of life when you wake up to a desolate place
It will knock you off your socks
As you fluster around
With your internal duster
Trying to keep your house tidy
I've fallen out of love for the world
Trying to wipe the slate clean
I've done this many a time
Green for good
Grey for bad
Try the catering rule
Never mixing the two
As you know what will happen
Poisonous food
Poisonous thoughts
It was only a dream
It feels like a nightmare in real life
When it comes knocking
Like a boat ready for docking
Don't follow
Don't copy
As I can get really stroppy
I've fallen out of love for the world

Natural disasters
Humanitarian relief
I can't understand the grief
How do I get the confidence to fight back?
Stack against stack
Day by day
My head will finally clear
I don't want any part of you near
How you dare
Is beyond repair
I'm not able to concentrate
As you try to plummet me into that delusional state
I know your there
Sitting comfortably in my rear view mirror

Written 2/8/2018

Save Yourself

Save yourself
Don't save me
Just leave me to work out my thoughts
It will make you sad
If I told you
Don't save me
Save yourself
You can go anywhere else
Just not be with me today
I will break the silence one day
If you hear me sniff
Just hold out your hand
Let me blow my tears away
I'm not being deceitful
I'm feeling relaxed around you
Don't save me
Save yourself
My thoughts have gone wondering
In the wrong direction
I will get back on track
I've done it countless times before
Leave me for a while
Don't try to make me smile
I'm feeling sad today
I'm working it through
I'm trying to save myself
I have things to look forward too
So that should be good news for you
Don't save me
Save yourself
I don't want to drag you down
To a dark remote and inaccessible place
I'm afraid you won't return
Save yourself before it's too late

Written 7/8/2018

Acceptance

I'm here again looking at the bare walls
I can hear the cat crying
Scratching at our front door
There will be nothing left in the morning
Only tale tale signs of life the night before
How do I feel?
I can't be bothered anymore
Complacency has kicked in
My acceptance is in tatters
Nothing really matters
Knockdown by knockdown
Punch by punch
Promising potential scattered out the window
How do you measure sadness?
When acceptance has been denied
I cried
Maybe I'm just a recovering depressive
Waiting for my next fall by the wayside
I'm looking at these bare walls
Wishing for inspiration
It feels different
They don't talk
They don't cry
They hold secrets
And never lie
They put up with my snoring
When I'm woken up at 2 in the morning
They move around especially in the dark
They're having a lark
To make a fool out of you
When I'm searching for the little girl's loo
Or tripping over my two left feet
Everything's different at night
Even the moonlight
Gives me a fright

Howling wolves chatter
It doesn't really matter
I could disappear in seconds
As the allure of the repressed shadow beckons
I've not got acceptance
If that's my penance
Dark turns to light
Everything that was alive
Stands perfectly still
If I can accept myself
Well that's half the battle isn't it?

Written 12/8/2018

Missed Connections

Story of my life really
I learnt about connections
Way to late
I would be more fulfilled if it happened earlier
I wouldn't have that nagging voice
Which didn't give me too much choice
Was it nature's way to encourage me to be different?
On that high step with lights stating don't be like her she'll never win
Chuck her in the bin
We can't connect with her
My missed connections getting more difficult
As I realise everything that went before was just a read through
I lost hope once
I lost time as life froze me out
The dark connected and that was all I could see
I ventured perishably close to suicide
Life and it's inequities we're dealt out
I missed that connection obviously
So has anything worked?
Which path have I forked?
Day by day different challenges
I can understand a schizophrenic wanting to keep their voices
As it's their only connection to make sense to move forward
I suppose through life's unfulfilling memories
We leap into internal intolerance
Trying to kick start life again and again
At what point do we take stock
And say this is how life is going to be
I don't think many of us will
Losing out isn't in our blood
It begins in the womb
Where we are cocooned
From everyday pressures

Written 13/8/2018

She Loves Me She Loves Me Not

I stare in wonderment
Unabashed by your beauty
Every essence I can see you have passion for life
For work
And for play
I stare in wonderment
That there is this person who gives so much of herself
Your wisdom and inner peace
Is awe inspiring
Yet you appear so delicate
I'm not ashamed to think like this
I'm not ashamed to have them in my dreams
They bubble up to the surface with me gasping for air
Sitting on the edge of reality thinking
I hope no one heard what I was screaming
I really wish I had your stamina
I really wish I didn't think
I makes it harder to be
Faithfully present when you're not around
My head goes wandering what we could be up to
You emanate a powerful brooding air
I just want one touch of your hair
It's what I want
It's what I can't have
Never in your life
I wish a lot of things
What I wish for is beyond my reach
I stare in wonderment
Where ever I go
Thankfully you are never there
I sit perched on a mountain cliff top
Picking daisy petals

One by one
They fly off into the wind
Each catching a breeze and floating off into the distance
Chalky white cliffs camouflage their beauty
She loves me
She loves me not
I never finish as the answer is always the same

Written 17/8/2018

www.ingramcontent.com/pod-product-compliance
Lightning Source LLC
Chambersburg PA
CBHW030155100526
44592CB00009B/292